Understanding Lenny

A Book About A Boy With Autism

Written By:
Natalie Abkarian Cimini

Dedicated To L & L

Copyright 2022 By Natalie Abkarian Cimini - All Rights Reserved

No part of this publication or the information in it may be quoted, reproduced, or used in any form or by any means, electronic or mechanical, including printing, scanning, photocopying, or by any information storage and retrieval system, without the prior written permission of the copyright owner.

Individuals diagnosed with Autism Spectrum Disorder (ASD) have unique strengths and difficulties and experience characteristics of their disability in different ways.

Some may be verbal, while others may not. Some may have sensory challenges, while others may not. Regardless, all individuals with ASD are unique in their own way and require different levels of support and assistance.

This book is based on our own autism journey and real life experiences to provide children who are not on the spectrum a glimpse of what ASD is and how it can impact a young child.

I hope this book will also be relatable to other children with autism and hope they can relate to Lenny in one way, or another.

- Natalie Abkarian Cimini

When Lenny was a little boy,
He didn't like sirens or musical toys.

Sounds like vacuums were especially loud,
And it was hard to spend time in a crowd.

Birthday parties made Lenny sweaty,
The cheering and clapping were more than scary.

He wanted to hide and run away,
When it was time to sing Happy Birthday.

Watching TV wasn't that fun,
Would he hear a sound that would make him run?

Lenny was always covering his ears,
Often holding back his tears.

When Lenny started going to school,
Mama and Papa wondered if kids would be cruel.

Would they ask Lenny what he was doing?
Would this lead to bullying?

One day Lenny started wearing headphones, The children wondered what it was for?

What was Lenny listening to?
They wanted to guess and asked for a clue.

When Lenny wore headphones there was no music, Lenny was sensitive to sounds and autistic.

Noises were louder and could be distracting,
Things like tapping and even bees buzzing.

Being autistic isn't anything bad,
We're all different, even a tad.

Some kids with autism don't say very much,
Others are bothered with a slight touch.

Sometimes Lenny smelled things far away,
They bothered him and ruined his day.

Sometimes he needed to change his shirt,
The tag was itchy and even hurt.

Lenny often repeated his favourite words,
Things about space and types of birds.

Some days in school he needed a break,
A quiet room, just to escape.

School assemblies in gyms were hard,
Since Lenny heard noises near and far.

That's why his headphones helped him a lot,
Since autistic children heard sounds others did not.

Lenny had feelings like everyone else,
He wanted a friend, but needed some help.

Including Lenny in games during recess,
Was what helped him really progress.

The boys and girls were so very kind,
They never judged him, or left him behind.

They seemed to know just what to do,
To help Lenny feel included too.

He may have good days and bad days too,
But that's ok because he has a friend like you.